AF504478

Candy
& Veronica's Visit

Written by: R. Elaine Chaklos

Illustrations by: Virginia Humphrey

Candy is definitely not ordinary. She is not ordinary with anything. She wears cool clothes and sometimes even flowers in her hair. Like all youngsters, Candy likes to experiment. Sometimes she plays dress-up. She might wear mascara and eyeliner to make her big, blue eyes even bigger, and a hint of wild rose blush to give herself a wholesome, healthy look. Sometimes she even wears her mother's clothes and high heel shoes just for fun!

Today, she is trying out nail painting. It's easier for cows because their nails are so B-I-G. As a matter of fact, she has to buy the large, economy-size nail polish, or she runs out before she is done with all her nails.

5

While Candy's nails were drying, her young friend Veronica came over to visit. She was pouting and rubbing her knee. What's wrong," Candy asked.

"I was hurrying and tripped coming across the creek on my way over here," replied Veronica. "My knee hurts." Her face puckered, almost ready to cry.

"Do you want me to punch you in the nose so your knee won't hurt so much?"

Veronica looked at Candy and started to laugh at the corny joke even though she still wanted to pout awhile. "No," she whined.

"Ok then. What about... knock knock," smirked Candy.

Veronica looked at Candy, then pouted a little and smiled a little. "Who's there?"

"Mooooo." (Just like a cow.)

"Mooooo who?" Veronica asked, starting to feel better.

Candy said, "Don't cry." Then she laughed.

Veronica snickered and gave Candy an exasperated look because it was an old joke.

Then Candy again said, "Knock knock."
"Who's there?" Veronica asked, now feeling quite a bit better.
"Wau."

"Wau who." Then Veronica realized what she just said and laughed.

Candy said, "Wow! I see you really like my joke."

Veronica rolled her eyes and said, "Oh brother."

"Just one more knock, knock joke, ok? Knock, knock."

"Who's there?"

"Juan"

"Juan who?"

"Some Juan who loves you," Candy said sweetly.

Veronica smiled and gave Candy a hug.

Candy's nails were dry by this time, so she asked Veronica if she would like to have her nails painted, too. Veronica did so Candy used a bright Happy Apple Red.

13

While getting her nails done, Veronica told Candy what happened in school that day. Veronica had a little trouble in calftergarten. She is an only calf and hasn't really learned yet how to play nicely with the other calves. The teacher, Miss LaLeche, says Veronica is doing much better now than when she first started school, but once in a while she still has a bad day.

Veronica didn't want to share her farm playset, so a couple of the calves in her class called her Veronica the Harmonica. She didn't like it one bit!

Veronica said with a pout, "Sometimes those other calves can be so mean."

Candy just listened and kept painting. Finally, Veronica got over her pouting and watched Candy dipping the paintbrush into the polish and swiping it on her nails, dipping and swiping, dipping and swiping.

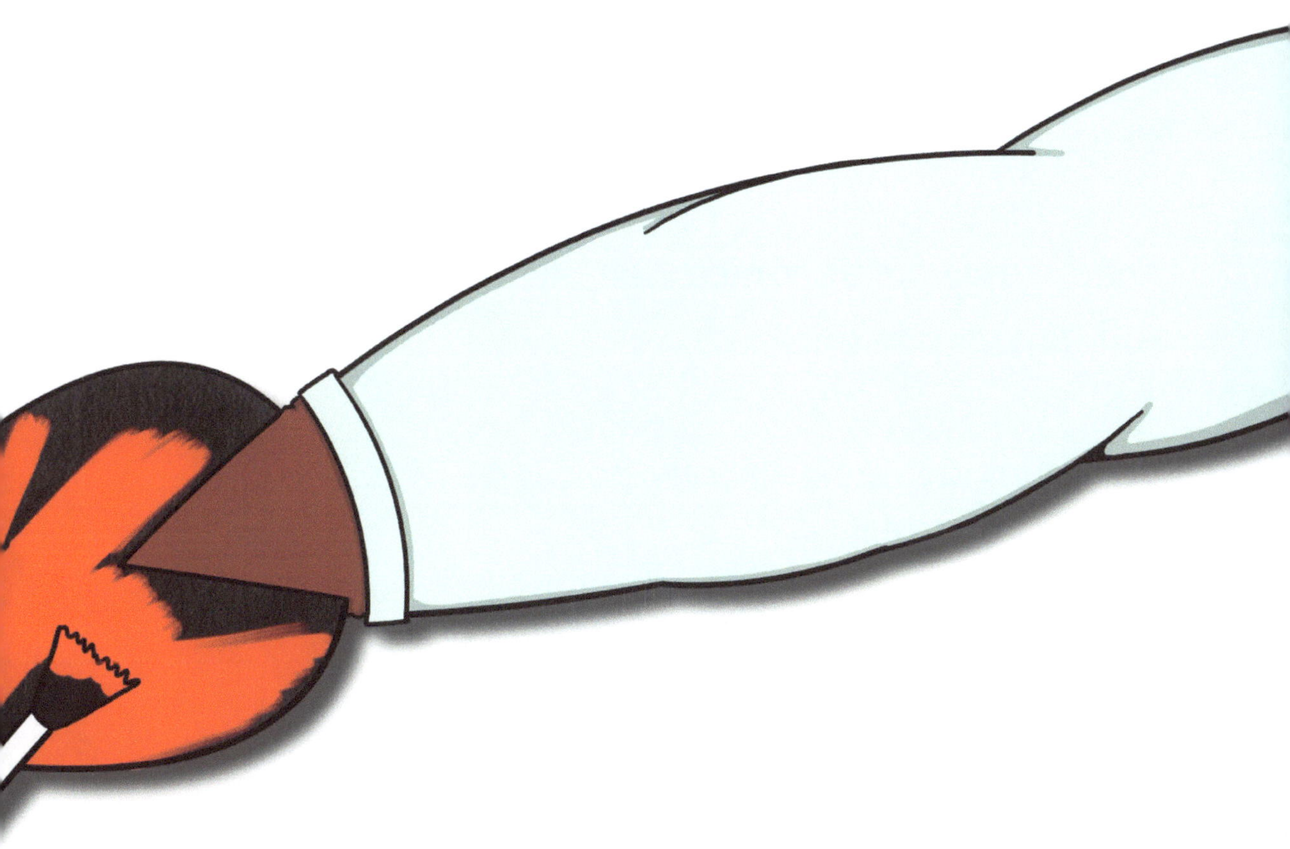

"Are you feeling better now?" Candy asked after awhile.

Veronica tilted her head to the side thoughtfully and said, "I think so."

"Would you like me to paint a few decorations on your nails?" Candy asked Veronica. "I've been experimenting. See."

Candy showed Veronica her own nails. "I think they will look great on you."

Veronica enthusiastically nodded. "Yes!"

"How's that, sweetie?" Candy asked when she was done painting little yellow smiley faces over Veronica's red nails.

Her small friend got a big smile on her face and said, "Super cute!" She likes to express herself just as Candy does. "Thank you," she said appreciatively and started to give Candy a hug.

Candy backed away, "Whoa! You need to let them dry or you will smudge them."

Veronica sat back down on her stool and patiently blew on her nails.

Candy took this opportunity to share her wisdom.
"Well, you know, the reason there is a sad is
so there can be a happy. If you didn't feel sad
sometimes, you wouldn't know that happy makes
you feel so good."

Veronica looked at Candy, then tilted her head and thought a minute. Then just like a light bulb turning on inside her head, her eyes got bright, and a big smile spread across her face. Veronica said, "Awesome!"

Just like a lot of little kids who look up to a
bigger sister or brother, Veronica was a copy
cat to Candy, whom she loved like a sister.
Candy said "awesome" all the time. And Veronica
thought that what Candy said about sad and
happy made a lot of sense.

"My mother said I could have a sleepover tonight," Veronica then said with pride.

"So I heard," snickered Candy, "Get it, so I herd." She was a good one to tease and make jokes. Then she tousled Veronica's hair and smiled.

"You probably better get on home now. Your mother will want you to eat and get cleaned up before your guests arrive."

Veronica happily skipped home being very careful not to smear the smiley faces on her beautiful red nails.

Candy loves doing nice things, it's part of her nature.

Color Candy and Her Friends

Candy

Henrietta Hen

Carrot & Celery

Wooly Bully

Learn more about Candy and her friends and download free coloring pages at www.candycow.net.

Veronica

Candy's adventures...

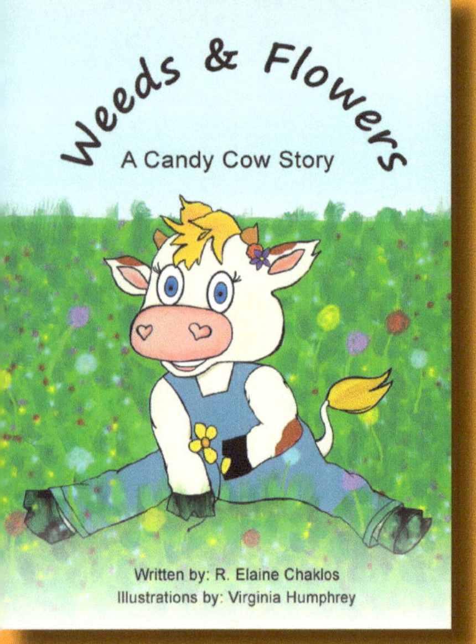

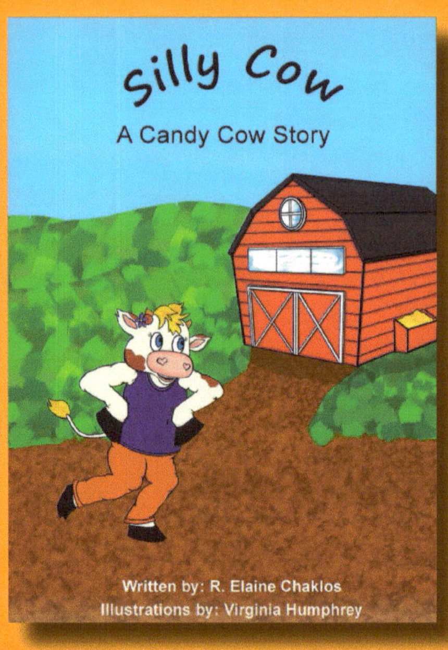

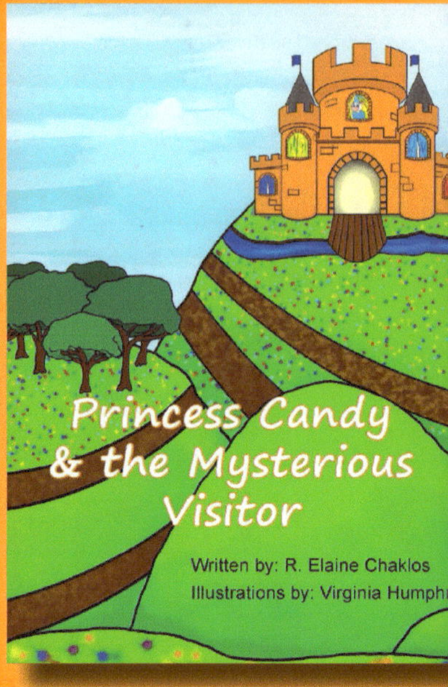

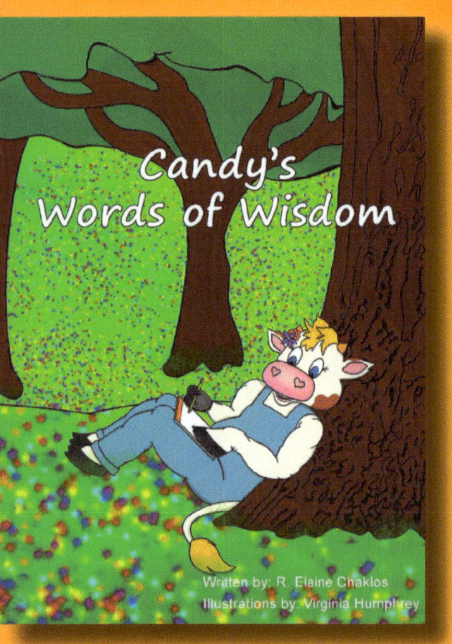

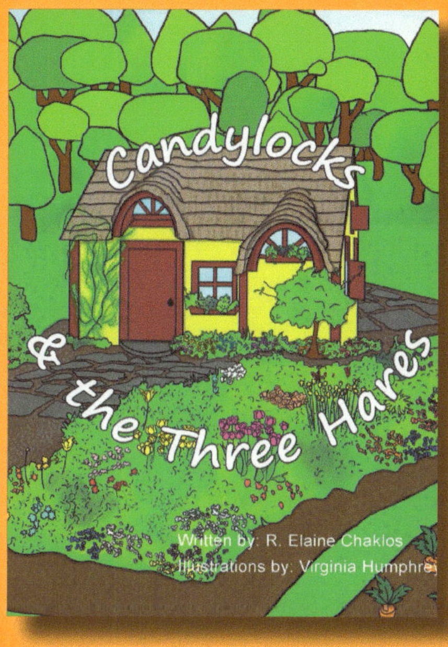

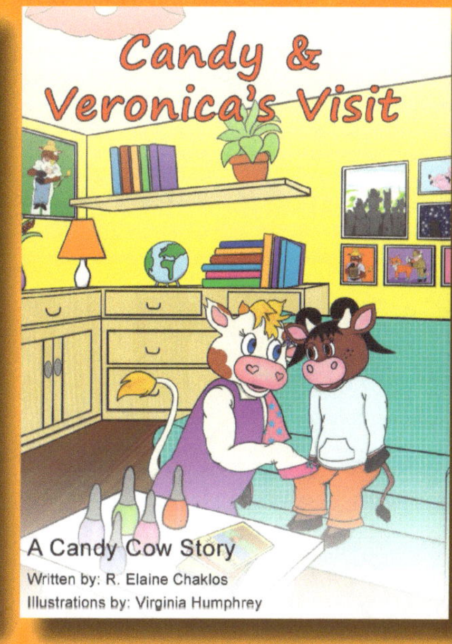

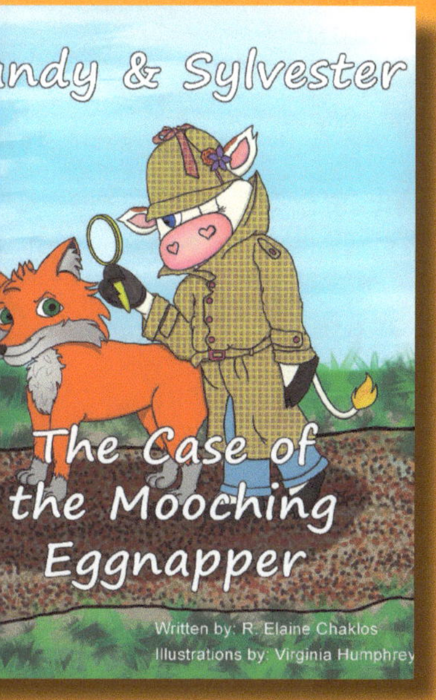

Most of Candy's books have an underlying moral: be the best you, you can be, be what you want to be, no one can make a fool of you without help from you, share, play nice together, etc., but some are just fun.

They are written to make kids and parents smile.

See all of Candy's stories at www.Amazon.com.